Porky £3   3¹/₂₃
52

Dinosaur Point

Paul Mills' previous publications

poetry
North Carriageway (Carcanet 1976)
Third Person (Carcanet 1978)
Half Moon Bay (Carcanet 1993)

drama
Herod (performed at the Cottesloe Theatre, 1979)
Never (performed at the West Yorkshire Playhouse, 1995)

Writing In Action (Routledge 1996)

Acknowledgements
Thanks are due to the editors of the following publications
in which some of these poems have appeared: *Dreamcatcher,
Exeter Prize Poems, The North*. 'Mile End Opera' was
commended in the Poetry London Competition 2000.

Dinosaur Point was the overall winner in The Poetry
Business Book & Pamphlet Competition 1999

Dinosaur Point

Paul Mills

Smith/Doorstop Books

Published 2000 by
Smith/Doorstop Books
The Poetry Business
The Studio
Byram Arcade
Westgate
Huddersfield HD1 1ND

Copyright © Paul Mills 2000
All Rights Reserved

Paul Mills hereby asserts his moral right to be identified as the
author of this book.

ISBN 1-902382-23-4

British Library Cataloguing-in-Publication Data. A catalogue
record for this book is available from the British Library.

Typeset at The Poetry Business
Printed by Peepal Tree, Leeds

Smith/Doorstop are represented by Signature Books, 2 Little Peter
Street, Manchester M15 4PS, and distributed by Littlehampton
Book Services Ltd, tel. 01903 828800

The Poetry Business gratefully acknowledges the help of Kirklees
Metropolitan Council and Yorkshire Arts.

Cover photo by Steve Crouch, from *Steinbeck Country*, published by Central
Coast Books.

CONTENTS

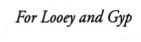

For Looey and Gyp

Dinosaur Point

Escaped from England,
driving miles to the far side of the mountains,
to where California, South of Santa Cruz,
reaches the vast San Luis Dam
like a sea at Dinosaur Point,

where hills of golden grass fold to a valley of visible dust,
all I wanted was us, and this – America,
as if we were some probe of an opening
panoramic discovery, like these hills
delivering us to sensation of new place.

But it was people you needed – dinner invitations.
Dinosaur Point – the name itself a Hot Spring
triggered my reading: *Basin and Range*,
yours *Tales from the City*.
So while I was writing my painted desert,
you grew more fictional and infringed.

And when it struck we had no antidote,
no anti-venom serum in our luggage.
While I got crazier about Snyder,
you read Adrienne Rich.
You were converted.
America was teaching us America.

Yard Plants

Sun-decks weathered by light
round that house in which we lived for a year.
That crimson creeper over the door,
stapled to hot wood,
those juice-red dark clusters of cups
crowding the walkway.
Tough thorns of it violent, tropical, Mexican.
The ivy on the telegraph wire
almost strangling those home UK voices
almost strangling each other.
And here too beside the Pacific
the underbrush was a growth
hidden, a thicket. We just cut through it –
innocents – as if the yard, the sun,
these plants, were ours.

News From Nowhere

Columns crack with gossip. Charles, Diana.
Pictures of her with handsome riding instructor.
Pictures of him solemnly smiling it off,
as if they were a couple just like us,
he on the far side of thirty, two nice kids.

So we think how lucky to be us and happy.
We are the way it should be. They are not.
Our kitchen isn't like their kitchen.
What's this on the cover of the New York Star?
Who's who in the latest Who's Who
of Fucking? Rage. Impotent
forefingered gesture at her supposed calm.
Cost to the Crown etc becoming mesmeric
in his eyes only and down his shirt-front possibly
in dribbles. Leaks out of the bed into the press.

Poor Charles. Poorer Diana. What's happened
to this marriage of innocents now that America
has its teeth in the sheets, is ripping them up,
searching for stains, truculence, depression?
Aren't we pleased we have a Republic,
Equality. Entertain friends. Innocence. Love each other.

Invitations

Once every month the Faculty Party.
Our chance to meet people.
People agree we make great entertainers,
though for the half-hour before
it's Faulty Towers. Videos for the kids.
Booze. Right tuck. Ignorant
of the politics we ask everybody.
Even those whose separations haven't gone public yet –
No one's told us. Even those the rest of the Faculty hate.

Parties as they used to be in this house –
Nick's, back in the 60s – Tell me about it.
Nude bathing. Nude practically everything.
The hot cooling off in their hot tubs.
Even nude eating.
Now the challenge is authentic Mexican cookery.
They all seem a bit tired.
Some a bit more married than they were.

And what do they make of us?
They are casting us as 'Englishman – boring,
married to beautiful English wife – beautiful,
and ten times more intelligent,
ten times more American.'
Probably they're right. I'm sure they're right.
The English thing after all is to say they're right.
The trouble is,
those who might be young enough to investigate,
already have wives, children,
and seem to be getting off quite well
on paternity, marriage,
just as we do ourselves, or seem to do.

What's happened to adventure, discovery, experiment?
The Beat Generation are quite baffled.
What's happened to intelligent, adventurous, beautiful
America? What's happened?
Why have they all gone and married the English?
Is only their speech different?

I know how powerful we are –
the hetero and reproductive couple
with the absolutely firm mind –
on this and any number of subjects.
Penetrating, infinitely impenetrable.
Arriving with green cards for sexuality.
Which will give us infinite invitations
to all other couples of the same sort –
the young ones, even the old ones,
even the ones who wish they were still married.

But how do we know, glass in hand,
whether we're talking to some lonely woman
or to one who thinks she's with her husband?
or when the gilt on the gingerbread's bitten off,
how dangerous it is to go on nibbling?

How do we know,
between the secret artillery,
what war on the Guatamala rug is escalating?
what naked back in the bathroom mirror
is that of an infidel strapped to its bomb?

The Hanging Man

The bolts in the wall
roar and a wall of air
opens the sides of the earth and so you
fly, with your parachute and reserve parachute
over Yosemite granite, over Germany,
over the jungles of Europe, Calabria,
the Neanderthal ridge. Air-born so
no country owns you yet. This is a place
unlimited, risked, and you soft
as nightfall you think, falling
like sunset, but you're rigged.

Ropes, knots, enzymes,
muscle-wall hanging
stretched, in your criminal position.
All this tangle gravity drags down.
Herculean white Adidas straps.
Codpiece, mask.
Accoutrements of muffled sense all gloved, clamped
in links and loops of perspex, grainless treads.
Punctual, though the target veers
to rock, flood, the early morning moon, ice-river,
avalanche, heat, derricks of Rotterdam,
concrete of Sacramento, swamp Amazon.

Where, when there's less and less soft material
will you choose your descent?
haul from its base in air with block and tackle
your pyramid-point down to a fine landing?
What do you sign your name to?

The planet slides beneath you, finger on spin.
Choose, choose your country, state, city.
Say what future you will perform there

which is not a matter of thin air.

How they line up, fly from alignment.
Europe, America. Where, where?
Sunlit Half-Dome, specific, jagged.

Stunt-man, Man in the Moon,
you have just one action to perform,
your noose, your chute, its simple cord,
as if more than a voice were talking you down
along this curve which is your flight's theorem
which is towards this smiling dolphin of stone
which is about to carry you on its back
about to vanish into a hole like smoke
out of which it once emerged like smoke.

And now you fly,
now with the huge
silk which will admit you.
Your transformation moves you over the trees.

Out of the blue like a cat
with a dazed early morning moth,
this is the moment, this the unscripted
present which will admit you,
springing at you inert
like a down feather, caught
by friction into a drop of shock.

And coming-to, it won't be long
before the place absorbs you,
Ukraine, The Schwarzwald –
wherever it is. Peru. Already
ants are running like words
across your papery skin,
entering every crevice in your head,
as if you're their homeland.

G.I. Joe

Tom, our son, aged five, is cruising the channels,
hitting on this, his favourite fix,
the mornings before Pre-School.
As always some psycho-mystical magician,
crazed by his own egomaniac drive,
sword-swallower out of old Europe,
who by lucky chance ingested a tank,
is now driving it unlicensed
over the innocent, the helpless, who have nothing.

That is – nothing but G.I. Joe.

G.I. Joe. G.I. Joe,
whose latest smart technology
is flying in with G.I. Joe himself, who is using it
as it should be used, in the name of Truth,
Justice and America – G.I. Joe Triumphant,
don't believe it. It's just a channel,
a manouevre. You can switch it.
G.I. Joe's just some kid American, helpless,
passionate for nothing, manic, frightened.

The Mission Of San Juan Bautista

'The voice of one crying in the wilderness.'

When Sister Agony came to stay
she called the children round her and told them a story.
How this land of theirs where they were born,
its streams of steelhead, shining water, rocks
and virgin forest, was Sin's property.

It was Sin who filled the breasts of their mothers,
filled the mountains and plains with wild game,
taught them to hunt. They hadn't heard this story
– Who was Sin? Then she made up a song.
'We are the children of Sin, of the land of Sin.'
Soon they were all chanting.

'But Sin is a cruel God,' she cried. 'Ugly.'
She held up her wise old hand. 'Stop. Listen.
There is a better God. The God of Love.
And once upon a time, Sin and Love
had a terrible fight. Whose side are you on?'
Some shouted out 'Sin!' Others 'Love!'
Some felt sick. The story was too frightening.

Then this old woman got hold of one of them,
a little boy, and threw sand in his eye.
'This is what Sin does,' she said, 'LIKE THIS.
It hurts, doesn't it! And sometimes it seems
there's no Love to protect you. Sin is stronger,
always ready to hurt and make you cry.
But Love is there. Love will wipe the desert
out of your eye. Love will make you see.

And from that time, everyone fought for Love.
Sin was defeated. Sin surrendered everything to Love,

all his eagle-feathers, fish and game, all his hunting,
all his land, every one of his children.
And all of them became the children of Love.'

The children learned this story off by heart.
The fathers and grandfathers turned sour.
There was a quarrel just as the old woman said.
And Love was victorious. Love, and friends,
Depression, Alcohol, Tuberculosis triumphed.
The battle filled cemeteries. No children, eagles,
only the empty sky, the broad desert, the heat,
and this church. And by the time we arrived,
guide-books to greet us – architecture.

Communion Hymn

The decanting of it, in white robes
at the altar. The breaking of it,
in lifted hands. The sharing of it,
equally, to the confirmed:
Vicar and Curate first, then the Choir,
then the small congregation, row on row,
Mrs Horrocks, Hilary, Eva, her mum,
wrapped and scarved against the ancient heating,
shuffle, partake, are blest; Sidesmen last.

Copernicus said: 'Heaven requires a map.
It's further than you think, so check your oil.'
In the meantime someone invented a bicycle.
I rode mine to church, sang duets
in the John Ireland Credo and Agnus Dei,
the same year that it was considered spiral
galaxies may be created by density waves
propagated across a galactic disk,
just before the confirmation of quarks.

I didn't believe in the sanctity of facts
but rather in the holiness of ghosts
in whose ruins I sang, the echo
lasting into the roof, each high note
a probe for excavation. Gloom made light.
God's voice before it broke, yet in whose chords
six-winged seraphs hovered, fiery pits
were dug for the idolatrous.
On the heads of Eva and Mrs Horrocks,
masonries fell, fields of burning corn
singeing their hair: Samsons,
Delilahs, Maries and Magdalenes,
pierced by the sword out of that Lamb's mouth.

It was all terrible but perfect.
No matter what blitzkriegs fell
from shuddering black fusilages,
emerging from their shelters this was safe:
this was the sacred refuge they returned to,
here under its silver and graphite sky
which drew around them, with a plotted line,
complete permanent circles of inclusion.

Ever and ever, however, was unreliable.
The whole story of what happened next
lay about like uncollected litter.
The Lamb's Book of Life was autobiography.
The stars lined up in rows to be discovered.
In place of the Absolute, a bubble of knowledge
expanding at the rate of confirmed facts
followed the same direction – into oblivion
taking the sun and outer planets with it,
each of equal inconsequence, a heat-death
of floating information, the same year
as the Cuban missile crisis.

And during one ultimate communion service,
the diffuse gloom of the building
was broken up. Everyone took some home
to their lives and deaths, wandered away
into their suburb estates, a taste
of tissue-paper on their lips, swallowing
the last replica of their God.

They walked hand in hand, two by two,
as if entering the ark, not to return,
the same year as strands of DNA
spiralled into frail gas-mantled gossamer,
the same year as the bones of hominids

came to light on the plains of African dust,
several years before the discovery of quasars
at or near the edge of the known universe,

and travelling like light,
fresh as the day my voice started to crack,
energy suddenly plugged itself to the wall,
started to dance,
rhythm burst out of the television,
cities filled with streets, streets with people,
at or near the edge of the known Pacific
as children from the age of New Wave
grew up with a sudden taste for colour,
particularly blue, also lemon zest,
not in heavy oil but sharp pastel,
not the arcane monument but the glimpse.

Complete with wallet, licence, passport,
a snapshot portrait of who they are
out of prehistory,
under the neutron sign, the sign of the spark,
the worshippers bowed down to let it come
towards them through the fingertip of a switch
as power washed across an entire
hemisphere visible from space,
cities luminous instantly in deadlight.
What happened to Mrs Horrocks and Eva?
A wind of photons
travelled through their hair, bones, consciousness.
Creation may or may not have had them in mind.
They went on being X-rayed in the grave
well beyond my thirtieth birthday.

The Pacific

Feeling afloat, still out there.
Somewhere we are.
Where? And with two children
who would tell us – Aptos, California,
Brighton Road. The road, house, path
to the sea between bleached house-boards.
Mummy. Daddy. Husband. Wife. Etc.

It's this Etc worries us. What has beached us
out of this ubiquity? this Hawaiian-
Japanese-Alaskan-Australasian space,
Great Lakes just inches above Florida
on a curve where slow lines plot themselves.

So vast it's like absence,
a surf-engine, working in no colour
except its own, invented with the earth's
future, running under cliffs as under itself,
about time perhaps undeceivable,
as about us who are just bathers in it.

Mono-coloured sails behind your shoulder,
resin-scent of eucalyptus bonfires,
out of that avalanche, that glacier, the ocean
glittering on you, you come to the sun
shaking with cold like a wave capsized
and spilled, hissing with joy.
The sand heats up.

Then,
next to me is your disappeared
imprint, scentless, gone again,
back to a trench deep as the Cordilleras,
some high zone of Equatorial snow,
its crests rolling, and maybe an upright hand
waves as you turn, facing our way, launched backwards
into the next crater.

Cabin

Making a right from Eureka Canyon Road,
the car grazes overhangs, twists uphill
through trees obscuring mazes
of slant heat, and somewhere above,
mountain-folded, our exchange partners' cabin.
Somewhere in the densely matted fragrance.

Make a right, follow the track to the Tomasens' ranch,
Tux and Elaine – nice people – she's an artist.
So much for directions. People I ask –
·no one's heard of anybody. They've no neighbours.
I stop by a house. The woman asks me in.
I could use her phone she says to tell you I'll be late –
has a mind to make me as late as possible. She's lonely.

More real-estate. A woman again
watches my car drive up, comes outside.
And while I go on mumbling in English English
but too friendly – disarmingly – of cabins,
she points herself towards me like a handgun,
keen to explain as if it's her only protection against rape
her away-husband's vision of the universe,
shows me his work-in-progress.

Shows me at last some hidden track uphill. I take it.
And now my directions make sense –
A fork in the path beside a water-tank.
A concrete tank, empty, in which I'll find
months ahead, in the heat of the new summer,
two racoons rotting with thirst and fear.

But as yet, no cabin. I'm lost up here.
A figure approaches. Black-haired, tanned,

Indian-looking. 'Puerto-Rico…' he shouts,
'And you from…?' – 'England.'
He shakes me with his heavy sweating hand,
anchored there in mist, the scent of sage
rising to a burning cone in the sun.

And then I saw the cabin.
A sort of wood-stack. Stove-pipe,
and Tux and Elaine's ranch.
And so, wading through hill-top brush,
I came to it at last. Deserted,
tumbling round itself but still a place.
From its decks was the miles-down still ocean,
stiller tips of green and madrone trees,
barkless, smooth, twisted and burned hard
in the mountain sun. A place of cones,
doorways, wilderness-rubble,
the whole hill-top's sphere a joined circle
between me, cabin and hushed forest.

So it was worth it – finding the place.
Cones, a handshake, deep drops of woods.
Then night fell suddenly like a tropic
as trees thickened, my chilled spine
tapering out all light, as wilderness came
towards me down paths half-memorised.

Rock-Salt

> *'The miracle of loving what dies.' – Albert Camus.*

The miracle of a girl who – at school
in summer in the twenties,
dawdling with her friends in a brine cavern,
among the carved passages under the fields –
after getting back late one afternoon,

was ordered to talk to the class about rock-salt,
and did so, amazing herself and them –
the miracle ablaze in her as she spoke,
as she speaks now about her granddaughter,
who inherits the shape of her eyes,
for whom the world is also ablaze, lit
with the miracle of friends and her friends'
friends, who know nothing at all about rock-salt.

Miracle of the sea,
brine-white sand. Miracle
of summer, the roasting sun.
Miracle of the smells of the bodies of friends,
Albert and Didier and Marconi in Algiers,
born the same year as my mother who never knew them,
moving among the shining leaves of ficus,
the warm wool and faecal smell
Didier carried around with him,

while the same summer, the same moment,
for her it was the taste of salt,
it was the scent of heat,
sweet drinks, liquorice,
river-mud under the schoolroom window.

The delicious sea outside the schoolroom door
of Albert and Didier, children in class,

in different countries, clothes,
an odour of joy, sometimes of rage,
beauty, and its second face, distress,

dissolving, like crystals in brine, to memory,
and launched on the river outside my mother's classroom
were ships that reached Algiers smelling of mud,
just as those from Norway smelt of wood,
just as those from Germany smelt of oil,
as more intense the sun heated the city,
grinding plaster and stone to a fine dust.

To those now dying who were children,
children in school, children in the sun,
who never met because of the tenuous drift
of a world still local in its extremity,
I say it was a miracle you lived,
that you lived on and beyond that summer
into a world luminous as those fields,
rivers, streets like overheated
corridors, leaves of ficus,
smells of bodies of friends,

that you lived on with friends,
lovers, children,
remembering eyes of the same
dissolving colour, the miracle
of chance and strange silk,
miracle of brine,
miracle of death.

And of a girl
now an old woman,
with difficulty undressing herself
for the process. The difficulty

of the no-less adjacent
but real and surprised wonder
of life going,

of trying to recall,
in delayed passages of speech

as if for her unpresent friends
instances, facts, this, that,

dissolving, luminous
words, miracles,
bits and pieces, rock-salt.

Mrs Pool And The Bowling-Green

On certain nights when a full
moon reared across the rigid
infirmary chimneys, Mrs Pool,
wearing only her nightdress,
would walk out into the middle
of the bowling-green,
and stand there mad as a hare,

and then the next day at dinner-time,
Mrs Done would knock in the grate
to Mrs McIntyre next door –
Mrs Pool's walking again,
look out for the children in case she talks.

It seems people was either mad or sane
in the nineteen twenties.
On moonlit nights
on the bowling-green
there were no shades of grey.

Attacks
seemed to come from within Mrs Pool,
whose son worked for Pilkingtons Glass,
and were inspired
not by violence at all just by shadows,
or by the sea
on the sands of Dee
which everyone thought had withdrawn.

And the bowling-green –
where Mr Haddock lay down after his heart-attack,
as his wood rolled on and on,
lay down with staring eyes –

I think my grandmother's cries
from the house were heard there
as she lay in labour with my mother.

Whatever happened never happened
very far away from the bowling-green.
Under the moon
even the infirmary chimneys were glamorous
in the eyes of Mrs Pool
swaying their arms and necks and ghosts of smoke.

Evolution

Last night I saw Hiroshima under the bomb,
the same dream – And the features of my miscarried
twins, hands that reach from nothing towards blood.
And those others before them who died blind.
It should be alright to know that the war's over.
That this is England. Blue and radiant summer.
That I should be contented. Today the doctor called
with some news – a new drug. But am I ready?
Am I ready to fight for another life, lose it again?

It started yesterday, the fact of the news
seeping through to me. I wish for fecund dreams,
I pray for them. To the drug. To God. To the thing
at the centre. I try to imagine its cells of racing growth
getting ahead of the bas-reliefs, the hand-prints,
the animal ghosts in the cave, its brothers and sisters,
ones who never got born or came this far,
who disappeared into the wall like horses.
I feel it move as if it's seen those ghosts.

My husband can't comprehend, it's war between us,
just when this should feel like a stopped war.
He doesn't understand murder, emptiness, doesn't hear
what falls away from the narrow ledges of words.
He pads himself, brings back his sweating whites.
Except that night when the seep was actual blood.
He was kind then, he and the doctor pacing about,
drowning themselves in scotch and smoke as if war
again were right overhead – their most feared thing.

None understands what this inside understands –
that it inhabits a place of rumours, ghosts, whispers,
an unsafe house, that when it's born it will fall out of me,

a miracle, survived. It will gaze at us with relief,
a trophy at its captors, adjusting its sight,
and with a wobbling smile. I won't let its curiosity sleep.
I will show it everything in wonder: that there are
creatures and trees living and living, that it's alive
in a light-year wind, blown from the first explosion.

The Cabin in the Clearing

Back in the fifties,
flickering through our neighbours' TV screen,
each episode the same, not much story,
it was about an enemy who surrounds you,
like a forest with soft, irregular howls.
Tuesday each week I sat in that sunless room,
gripped by Yukon territory, vast Sub-Arctic.
The TV showed the interior of the cabin,
oil-lit – beds with bark still on them,
upright slots the size of letter-boxes
through which men in beaver-fur
would slide out the long rifle and fire,
fire and fire again at the masked forest
which never came close yet seemed still
to touch them with the hand of a Savage Devil.

The little screen was bluish, shrunk from the cold.
Those were the early years of Children's Hour
when we had no TV. So there I sat –
the firescreen embossed with sprigs of mint,
bookcase, bureau, fat old chairs,
arrows thudding into pine-logged walls of Yukon forest
aimed at men by men with painted masks,
arrows with fire alight so panic ran
through the women and children of the cabin
so that men climbed out, clawing at flame,
clawing at ice, while I imagined
the tops of the forest stretching across
the north of the globe like a lace antimacassar
merging with the tundras of White Russia.

Why were they there in the Yukon?
Was it for gold?

There are places deep in the far north
where no white man's foot has ever trod,
where there are no maps, and where, unknown to man,
strange tribes and beasts unseen by human eyes
roam through the trackless wild.
All I knew was smoothed by Movietone.
Home was with the pale-faced round our hearth,
its fireback where sparks burned in the soot
ragged as forest, spreading glimmers over the black
like cities on a chart of the world's clearings,
then one by one went out.

Poets

We knew they were there.
The place was saturated.
Throw a biscuit out of a window, you'll hit a poet –
MacCaig in Scotland said that. It's true here too,
their published works collecting on Nick's bookshelves,
waiting to be unread.
My trouble is – I've read them. And here they are, WASP
to a man, staring at me with a kind of adamant, presidential
profile cut in stone.

Poets who know their own back yards down to the last pelican-feather,
creeping up with bugged stealth on the mating calls
of the yellow banana slug. Nature – Precious subject.
One more little thing for them to possess.
I'm amazed, I tell them, that this land ancestral to the Ohlone
should become the subject of prize poems, pot-sized poetic
prize agriculture. Pumpkin pie poetry. Isn't it stealing?
They don't like this at all. I'm porcupine, skunk,
'And Long Live Walt Whitman!' – shouted out, drunk –

You're doing better.
This after all is Mary Eagleton's party – revisiting
her American exchange; you're in better company than I am.
1986, and a soft inland in-flowing tide of new, intelligent,
careful reappraisal has your hearing, yours has theirs –
women together. You are liking what it is you learn.
And what is new. The world seems to be moving
in your direction, moving fast.

And yet what I'm trying to tell you,
especially you but also everybody else
is that the Earth is five billion years old,
is that we've lost our need to speak with it,

that this is more important than anything, that our future
is resting on a crust of progressively frail increasingly dangerous
misunderstanding, that issues of gender seem comparatively
irrelevant. You don't like this at all. I'm porcupine. Drunk.

Jealous.
And it seems to you I've fallen out with everybody,
especially you, and that you don't like this – married to some
perverse raving drunk secular manic religious atheist
shouting out about Feminism, Masculinity, Nature, the Ohlone,
who can find no fit for himself anywhere,
who disagrees with you about the future,
who doesn't like you, doesn't like you at all.
Nor do you like driving this person home, sleeping with it.

Two Women and a Persimmon

'We've only to look at each other and we conceive,'
she's saying. 'Even if our night things meet in the tub...'
Outside on the unkempt grass, it's evening,
rear of their house by the river,
you and she beside a persimmon tree,
unsurpassed by its beauty, juice of twilight.

Inside, I'm helping her husband draft his novel,
about an outsider, maverick with a wife and four kids,
who'd rather meditate than teach literature.
But there's the rent, the overdraft.
The place is a mess. Manuscript.
Stuffing out of chairs. Chardonnay. Toys.

You don't rate him much. It's she who's invited us,
especially you, you think – women together,
women whose intelligences connect.
Her marital racket's not what you had in mind,
nor this rapt visit to the persimmon, rounded fruit
glowing with harvest sky. 'And spermicide's useless,'

she's saying. 'After Blaze... he's such a hyperactive.
I don't know...' as Blaze aims his low-level model bomber
over the grass at the geese, an innocence
neither of you admire. 'And what about you?' she asks,
'Will you have more?' The question spreads
around you like dark oil.

'I taught history at college,' she goes on. 'The Quakers,
wonderful, you know – *O thou North of England,*
out of thee did the branch spring and the star arise
which gives light unto all the regions about.
But what they meant were the roots surely.

That's what all these leaves and stuff are for.

Don't you agree – making good roots?
Why should trees see it our way up?'
You smile at each other. The questions have suddenly
become complicated, more and more treacherous.
At first you think it's because you hate metaphors.
But it's roots – it's that reference time and again to roots.

The Bridge

The day we chose to let America show us its first city,
north from Santa Cruz, Half Moon Bay, Pacifica,
driving the coast route to the Golden Gate,
out of the fog, our glimpse of it
was of two swaying masts, a pilot craft
moored to San Francisco,
towing the whole city out of harbour,
ready to break free, cut loose, vanish
into a river of light.
Other ships were moving fast upstream,
a floating Toyota factory out of Japan.
Out on the flat shining plane of the bay
Alcatraz like a cubist mirage.

Downtown crowded us with streets, steepness,
the entire city a huge lift to the top
of the Trans-America Pyramid and its window, like thick
aquarium-glass, as if the gold of the sun swam in America.
Houses flung on the hills like litter. Every space used up.

We were exhausted. We ate on high stools lined up in front
of a mirror in a restaurant bar. Nobody spoke.
Nobody spoke to us. We drove home, an hour and a half's drive
by the open sea, in the mood of someone trying to come round dazed,
not coming round, as if the click hadn't worked
and we were still there, except we were here back at home,
trying to fill up the spaces of home – of the rest of the evening,
of the night. You were ready to get on the phone quickly,

calling your friend for an intimate stir of English hometown
gossip, listening for new playbacks in her voice,
while I wrote my notes for the next day's class,
British Literature up to Sixteen Hundred,

not enough time to rearrange my mind.
And the children –
running about and urging on each other's ridiculous screams –
Hide and seek. Where am I? Where are you?.
There's no mother or father in this house. Only screams.
So when one particular scream, especially elastic, stretches out,
will not stop stretching out, I snap.
I am wanting it hurled back in its room like a boot-scuffed rug.
The fact that it's in its nightshirt doesn't deter me –
it is a scream on the run. But then it falls, then it is a silence.
She shows me her arm that's hit the radiator
bent back on itself –
not with a scream but a whimper, 'What have you done?
What have you done now?'

What's happened to San Francisco?
All that's dark.
Together we examine her botched arm,
the bend in it. This is Night.
The nurse in the clinic is asking, 'How did this happen?'
The bone surgeon is quizzing, 'Who did this?
What do I answer? What's the aesthetic? –
That happens shows what you don't know
but discover later.

And it was weeks later, the cast removed,
walking back together in the carpark,
that her hand, rushing up, seized mine.
All she knew was my hand adrift in the air,
into which hers came and stayed suddenly.

Déja Vu

Early morning sun.
The day is bracing.
There's some wind in the trees.
The fog moves.
You're at the mail-box down on the dusty road.

A letter from England?
Yes, there is.
Popped inside those bundles of glossy junk.
Your name on the envelope
in my handwriting
– strange,
since I'm asleep in the bed you just left.

A letter from your husband asleep in the house.
You tear it open.
It's a letter
written to you from years into the future,
written from now, just as I am writing this
now.

What's happened?
You start to read.
You stop.
You can't go on.
This is dissection.
You are being folded out like a map.

What will happen?
Passion Cancer
Divorce Career
Pregnancy What?
What?

The letter is reassuring.
The children are well.
It hopes you are.
Where are they?
Have you left us?
Yes.

Yes.
And other news.
A war in Europe.
Public and private deaths.
We've had such storms.
The ice is melting.
It rambles. Little details.
Then an entire paragraph on the cat.
Then best wishes. Love.
And the children? Yes,
Yes, they send theirs.

The children get up, get dressed, you drive them to school.
They think you are a little bit distant this morning,
a bit preoccupied, entering freeway lanes
as if reading something, while the heat
presses the metal roof and you open a window
into the oncoming draughts as you move forward.
You have folded your letter back in the envelope in your head
where it will continue not to exist.

The Woman Poet

Are we in love with the woman or with the poet?
And which of them is talking about recipes?
Each of us is such an idiom-borrower
there could be thousands of us in this room,
not just three talking about poetry.

'The best is when the poem speaks itself,'
she says, 'so writing's a form of listening.
Like love it's hard to do it alone.'
'But what about...'
'Audience? No problem.

The poem speaks and you are its first listener.
The poem isn't speaking to you alone,
nor in your voice alone. So most of our worries –
that it might be too personal, intimate, or
not personal, intimate enough, or untrue –

don't let any of that waste your time.
Listen, then *write*. Poems,'
she's saying, 'mustn't be interrupted.
All we do is make sure we're around
in those places where they like to be.'

You smile. The oracle is uttering.
'But what places?' I say. 'Whole stories?
What if I don't want... aren't accurate enough...
even too accurate?' She laughs. 'Not your problem.
Or if it is the gift will find its way.

You're losing your trust.
It doesn't always do what you think it will,
won't always be where you think it is.

And if it seems to you to be biding its time,
that's because mistrust is a form of fear.

It is afraid of you and you of it.
Let me tell you something. Listen to me.
It is home, wherever home may be.' After which
the conversation continued more rapidly.
Recipes... armadillos... Then she left.

A Piece Of Cake

Their house seems a peculiarly English house
from the outside, pebbledash porch,
solid brick not wood. Only the hills surrounding say
that this is California. The heat
cheap, quake-scorched. The San Andreas
not that far off like a sulky feeling.

Her sister's married to one of the Pogues.
Not the one so drunk he can't even sing his own songs.
One of the others.
And she's married to someone so taciturn
we can't even tell what nationality he is.
Hungarian-Irish? Scots? A sort of Serb? Nobody knows.
He hardly speaks. But she's in love with him, she's so in love.

They play Leonard Cohen together,
moving together like parts of a catastrophe.
We are here – you, me, our children, their children,
and your brother, staying with us,
the one who wants to import himself
to the top of the Silicon range,
who's already faxed through his CV.

Here for dinner.
You and she have been comparing marriages.
It's a hobby natural in this parts.
After such aerobics, dinners follow.
How she's fixed herself up with somebody so inscrutably
unpleasant, possibly violent, interests you,
possibly interests her. What's it about?
You've already visited your mutual friend's on and off relationship

with a ranch, a husband, children,
who wears on her car a *Mothers For Crack* sticker.
After dinner our hostess brings us some treats –
specially prepared. Her husband smiles.
'Try these cakes. See which ones you like,' she says.
We try some. All they taste of is cake,
what's the problem?

What's the problem? Driving back
the problem is we can't stop – can't stop giggling.
Then, back in the house, it's a laugh,
it's a scream, the children can't get to sleep.
You and your brother and me and those cakes.
What did they bake in those cakes? We raise the roof.
Overcome by marriage, brotherhood, freedom and spastic joy,
we scream, embrace, and shed such tears of absolutely nothing.

Californiana

    for Jim McCord

Cliche-abundance – the constantly ripening
stacks and squash of produce,
armies of cabbages in fields – you can't call them
fields – more like vast cemeteries behind wire,
penitentiaries of fruit. Everything planted out
under gene-surveillance. Into the mould
of Brad, Chuck and Happy,
vitamin-rich in-pourings of muscle.
Each suburb street a backdrop shot
for some awful man-and-woman thing,
or for genocide. As if we cared
more than to say – where's that city?
do we recognise it? were we there?
America trying to run away from itself in high heels,
still in seductive silk, tearing it off,
trying to become abject, original, naked,
reversing at high speed
out of the car-lot. Get away. Get away from all this!
No escape for mogul man's
quick-drop change of gear, girls, reflectors,
nor for the sucking thrusts of mosquito
oil-pumps: Hollywood, Universal,
all those millions of gallons of gas and blood,
running in one single-system engine,
nine million drivers at the wheel.
Sorties of cliches loosed on the Santa Ana
buzzing in swarms. But even the corpse isn't dead,
it must return, pick up its lost life.

Misanthrope

I'm meeting one of my students – Steve – in a bar.
He's an actor and gifted: his performance
in Harrison's *Le Misanthrope*
at the little Santa Cruz Theatre
impeccably renders the opposite of himself.
Abundance, talent, future: he has it all. And yet,

some barrier. He won't be drawn.
Something. What is it?
He tells me that his wife is going blind.
I am staring at the grille of a Zodiac
fixed to the front of a restaurant on Main Street,
brilliant steel, a stunt beast of the Fifties,

now an advertisement,
a going-places God, ubiquitous, gregarious,
a bit like Steve should be who knows he's not,
or can't be now, yet no Misanthrope either.
Today they've seen the guide dog she will use.

What does it mean going blind in America?
What if the ear is the rim of a deep canyon
into which little or nothing whispers?
Can it be trained? –
Will all-visual America become speech?
Wherever she goes, will it
change itself into sound and touch?
Is it loss that's diagnosed or increase
of attachment?

It is loss. Steve's too. He is preparing
for a foreseen catastrophe – his, hers.
He has already discovered a voice
through which he is training himself, making
himself ready for this new, undirected, unknown role.

Power

Gradually,
on some days,
after several on and off stops and starts,
you feel it begin to flow into you from people,
from this place, your students, your teaching,
ideas. What is this thing?

Power. Something to do with women,
being a woman,
the education of women by women.
And when you're on the phone to some woman particularly
mature, intelligent, also especially lost and adrift,
I hear it –

Power. Grave and awkward.
Each of you is a diver into a wreck,
without maps, or with charts you'll discard.
I notice your face altering, and your body
like an anatomist's map – terribly open,
labelled by men – wrongly.
Now you have new labels, new words –

Yet on those days when your power deserts you,
when you feel worthless and awful inside,
I am there to comfort you, rearm you – the wrong person –
a sea-eagle carrying its prey back to its mate in the nest
while you're keen to be loaded with explosive.

You are Delilah cutting off Samson's hair,
then doing everything else for him as well,
everything for everyone. Felling the temple
round his ears – you can do that too
while you cook, entertain, teach the children,

can't stop teaching, can't stop teaching yourself.
There's so much. You can't stop becoming powerful.

And back from America, it's in our luggage.
You've brought it with you. So that, one night,
while I'm out with a friend for a drink
and you join us, stay some minutes then leave,
it is power, the fume of it in your absence,
a new gravity – we feel it – its coolness, pallor,

lightness, its sex, its allure
of having nothing to do with any past,
only with that by which it acquired itself,
wanting more of itself, determined to get it,
power having become its only supply.
And you'd found a supplier, not in us.
It was all about how you wore your coat,
how you really had to be somewhere else.

Ice Stations

Feathery seeds adrift in the earthquake hills
over Yosemite shadowed by masks
of bark, juniper, lichen, staring
at the granite-hooded mountain,
sliding into dark the car lights probe
seeming twin and equal as we move –
Don't you trust my hands
to steer us through, turning, turning
up and up this corkscrew of a road?
We've left the soft climates behind,
below. This is tundra. Cool,
bluish, the last of the sun
foaming into ice and survival territory.
What's happened now to the meadowy river,
million-leaved screes and rafts of sequoia?
We stop, get out, walk on a stage of stone,
top of a two thousand foot rearing cliff,
levelled greys and folded-up summits,
a Scandinavia high above the Pacific.
Ninety degrees of heat on the valley floor,
while up here trees crawl in the night,
huddle until the rim of sunrise
flares to keep just toughened things alive,
holds their scent maybe a few hours.
Here there's simply peaks and troughs of rock.
The sky brushes us with a lack of attention
bending spines to the wind.
Out of sight, somewhere, we should be –
in a street where figures overlap,
lose themselves, blur, in their night-shopping.
Standing by this air-fall into silence,
what we said to each other is still here,
frozen over branches leaning out,
footprints caught in a drift like those
in Beverly Hills sidewalk cement
left by the stars, their names zoomed
from studio-starred backdrops just like this.

Sierran

The river was elsewhere, wasn't within us,
or there were two, flowing from the same peak.
Instead of rapids tumbling to slow effacement,
you were the falls, the most sudden descent,
the veil ruptured in mist and inhaled
chaos where no memory is exact,

where in a flood of quick succession,
skimmed on the air, absence succeeds absence.
I should have known that you were moving at speed,
that rock was your impediment,
that you had decided in favour of water,
that each line was always going to be throwing itself

helpless into the next,
that you were in free fall,
that you didn't want to be held and steadied towards
safely piloted landings in cramped dusks,
suburbs skimming towards you,
that you'd rather drown in your own escape.

Photogenesis

Beginning with families,
each learning its history without fear –
yet who can tell it?
Searching a drawer at my mother's,
where she might have put some money somewhere,
so old now her hands forget themselves,
I find these photographs sent home from America,
years ago. Mostly, they're of the children,
seven and five. And looking at them,
then back at these words, which is the story?

Dark words, bright pictures – an oasis of happiness.
Eucalyptus – taste that scent – a constant drizzle of light
around our house just yards from the Pacific
where a freight train ran twice a day with its WAUWA
klaxon, where two children stand like *Stand By Me.*
Or in Disney, riding in a teacup.
Or in a kitchen of mothers and birthday cake.
Each room pinewood and sauna-looking.
Then Dinosaur Point, impossibly blue,
out on a planet that is and isn't Earth.

Every moment sun-oiled,
except this one of my mother in an Indian blanket
wrapped on a cold beach by a driftwood fire
visiting us just after my father died.
And people were understanding.
They were nice people we met here.
Whatever it was linked them with their names,
each of them was trying to steer it through.

Nor was our time with them a searchlight surveillance.
Or if it was it picked up friendliness mostly.

The holstered gun of the State Park Warden
didn't suppress his smile the day of the picnic,
the day before we left.
And there were smiles everywhere, your smile
which seems to have lodged itself in the children permanently.

On the reverse of one you sent my mother in 1986 –
'Outside the Spanish Mission at San Juan Bautista.
L and T are wearing genuine Red Indian headbands.
I don't know what the owl is doing.'
Lucy at Disneyland – her arm in plaster.
Tom, aged five, in the temple at Mitla,
little kneebones touching, a bit smallish
in the big space of an Aztec worship site.
Then this one of the Golden Gate Bridge in transit.
All another story, a better story.
From print to print – two children – the shared
and priceless outcome of our marriage,
and in the background, all that blue
rising into a haze.

And tonight, bringing these photographs home,
aged fifteen, seventeen, they seize on them,
they are delighted by them. This was our life
and still is our life,
this is the wave-tip of it, the surf of it still
glittering, glistening in them
as they shuffle the instants of it together,
looking at it, as if this were the story and maybe it is,
maybe I told it wrong. Like cameras,
words too have a powerful click mechanism.
The borders are open, frontiers indistinct.

Flight Back

Before we fly home our minds fill up
with England again, with mud.
This sludge-clump out in the North Atlantic.
A sticking-together, single-voiced, single-city
integrity – World At One.
Arterial London clogged with breathless air.

But we don't even have that. We're regional.
North Yorkshire – province of a province.
Our exchange partners – sun-loving –
even they've spent half their year in Greece.
Here the only heavy traffic's the transportation of sheep.
Market the one tumescence every Thursday.

There's the Cathedral
yet having seen the Hopi men in their dance,
in the clear light of the mesa, on their earth –
why not knock it down, make it a car-park.
England would be getting what it deserved.
All its excrescences sluiced. So call in
the demolishers with their earth-moving equipment,

let them unpick all that stone re-echoing, preached
history, lay it out flat. Flat. Instead of depth
let there be surface, since the weather builds no building
solider than cloud. But as yet we haven't even arrived –
the plane's wing hasn't yet touched Ireland.

Back to it all – its credit sprees,
little postcard coasts, landscaped sky,
parliaments of the posh, cockney druids,
who's with who, who's seen what –
Kiss Of The Spider Woman – what we've missed,

can't catch up with, since the people we were
won't be returning, have been changed by a story
neither can tell – since there's nobody here can feel
the scent of sage-brush, of the night asphodel.

Northumbria

Driving out of the Lakes, East,
into the sweep of the North – Appleby, Brough,
Briggflats somewhere up there – the wonder of it,
suddenly I'm amazed that we live here,
along with these bedridden ghosts of time.

From Lindisfarne to Rome the tracks of St Wilfred
visible to these clouds, across these hills.
Stasis of Middlesbrough – upshot of smoke.
Smudge of York to the South.
Why am I still thinking of Arizona?

Why elsewhere when I want to be here?
Why does England seem like an interruption?
Something we should be learning to do without?
A pressure that's worked loose?
It could be comfortable but

tomorrow you might have moved forever.
I think of that approach to the Grand Canyon,
bordered by wild grass and wild fir, a stag
that stood in the road, no real warning
of where we were heading – and then the thing

seen through hotel plate-glass with people eating.
Our sight of Bright Angel Point lifted by cutlery
into speechless mouths, a feast to which
we were only adjacent. Not until we felt the heat
rising out of the gulfs like a strange wind

did we know we were there.
So what tells me I'm here now in Northumbria –
Land of the Prince Bishops. However beautiful

none of its ghosts rise from canyons
carved out of space and air.

There are no such deep holes in our island.
No such geology – just little wild places
of swamp and rock. Belief has cooled.
The sun's half-hearted. The boiling
of unbearable rock has stopped.

Even politics is a half-shadow,
content with moderate effulgence,
distances trying to hide the horror of suburbs.
Nothing sheers this island out of the blue.
What invigorates? What will make it new?

Hard Data

We argue in the bathroom, on the stairs,
down into the kitchen. We like arguing.
Science, gender, history – not what's proved
but why? by whom? And can there be such a thing
as hard data? Who scripts time?
What about earthquakes? – Or is it all
plastic, cool, relative surface-cosmetic? –
No. YES. And Why? Because... because

because it's only this will produce Freedom –
But this word so magic to you, to me
is just a four-wheel-drive Cherokee,
on its trip from showcase to breakers' yard,
dangerous to this thin envelope of air
easily pierced and certainly irreplaceable.
Freedom maybe on some junkproof Earth.

But for you nothing's irreplaceable. The concept
'Earth' is like the concept 'Hair' – it can be dyed
and should if by such means Independence
is signified – the right to drive up any mountain road,
be what you will and where. 'Hard data', you insist,
like 'Climate', 'Parent', what you will – Anything,

is in somebody's pocket. – Like 'She's blonde',
'He's lost'. All of them are statements
somebody owns – And so round the house
we go on and on arguing. We like it. It excites us.
Who's telling the story? Whose is it?
Into what hard data will it set?

Shadows

Across the stream where Angel carried Tess,
under Mr Rochester's attic window,
passing Mr Phillotson's schoolroom door,
gardens where lilies shone for Gertrude Morel,
she walks behind the shadows of other women,
from the lych-gate to the workhouse steps,
a short, lifelong distance.

She never met the one who would take her
out of here and away at the end of the story.
She has given up this and all other hope.
She rejected the sensible farmer who hoped.
She preferred the one with the flower and the kiss,
the unnavigable husband, shiftless thief.

And so this woman of rue walks through the town,
towards the end of our street, in jeans now,
she turns into it walking towards our house,
slightly more tipsy with misery than usual,
wearing her baggy sweater of distress,
a cemetery-stone shadow and avenger
coming against all those who've got off light!

Coming for you. She knocks. I let her in.
You hide upstairs, probably in the bathroom
where there are mirrors, where you can breathe,
re-invent yourself.
All you want is a new world of new faces.
Now she's telling me her worst memory.
Now there is this vulture in the picture.

You won't admit she's here. Or what you fear –
that when at last she drags herself back under

the buried streets of the town into darkness,
wrongs, misdemeanours, shadows,
whatever it is she carries on crushed shoulders,
she'll sink our whole house and you with it
under those haunted slabs.

She's the story
nobody wants to hear. You lock your door,
feeling the night, the town, the streets tighten,
whisper to Freedom *GET ME OUT OF THIS*.

Sponges

Absorbed into the softness of it again –
Marriage, our home, England,
into a place where nothing seems quite clean,
nothing just adjacent or skin-deep,
every built stone soft with past,
heavy with it, – every face spongy
even our own. Even our chipped
kitchen equipment memoried.
Surfaces eating into each other, saturated.
There is a space our eyes can't clarify.
Between things, between us.

Lovers again, but trying to be uncommitted,
as if we were not each other,
but we were. We had come home.
You had become a daughter-in law again
taking my mother out to some Great House.
And there was I sitting on her wrist,
like some hawk, slouched,
with spongy eyes. It was frightening
how much family I had absorbed,
how much I was married. So little left
for any sort of affair – even with you.
And not much time. The future
was opening its huge, spongy consistency.
How very lumpy it looked. Permanent.
How divorced from space, light, clarity,
adjacence.

English light, like staring through a stock-pond.
Old friendships crusty with each other.
I was parent. You had become a child –
restless, high, deprived and on the move.

Leaves

One month after we arrived home,
leaves started to fall from the twelve
pinnacles of the aspens
in our garden, into the river, across the grass,
among skeletons of others still unswept.
I looked up at their rustling broken connection,
branches stark, a family
of curves in ever-grey sky.

Then two months later the room
shook. A flower in a glass of water trembled.
I stared at it.
This can't be happening, this isn't
America – we've come home!
But it was happening. The ripple of a quake
in Wales, the same
familiar rustling curves of the earth
in that glass, under our old Cumberland stone hearth.

Then two years later you moved out.
Then it was a story we were in.
I couldn't speak until it finished.
You kept coming back.
You couldn't leave us.
Three years, four, five.
The leaves fell in the river, over the grass.
Not until it ended could it begin.

Ghostly

Last-minute students, rush-hours on the M1 –
every time, your journeys are made late.
It used to be every other weekend,
now one in three. It's understandable.
Neither of us can stand it.
Watching you here –
ghostly – as if we both connived in your apparition,
on the staircase – in the bathroom –
stroking the cat –
after your five, sometimes six-hour drive,
since there's nowhere else for you to stay,
how about a cup of tea and a chat?
For almost an hour you just sit,
you can't speak. Then your story begins –
loneliness, depressed maternal feeling.
Your single female colleagues can't understand,
hooked into their desks and research messages.
Your wife-and-mother acquaintances can't either –
why you left, why you keep coming back.
You sense you are being hissed from all directions.
What shall we say?
That when it comes to dates on chunks
of freezer food in unrecognisable shapes of ice,
hoover bags, yoghurt and dinner money,
you are out of this world. With each return
it's your children's skin, spirit, voices
you are needing around you, closer to you.
The motherhood you deserted wants you back,
won't be faked. And so you're here,
after each increasingly long absence,
here with your ex-husband, ex-kitchen.
We both understand, have to try to stand it.
Each of us is learning how to be ghostly.
Even our real voices have to know
that we're not here together but talking
out of another life.

Brenda

'Who's Brenda?' my bank-manager is asking,
his eyes on the item of £40 a week,
seeing some lavish fantasy on the side
eating the family budget.
When I give him the picture
he smiles – 'Cut it.'

In spite of the sink, slime on the washed-up
cutlery, we were thriving.
Yet you insisted we get some woman in,
some reliable substitute for you.
We interviewed one person and employed her,
matron in humour and girth, slightly insane,
a prison visitor who had married a murderer.
We found this exotic but she couldn't cook.

And you with her wasn't much of a fit,
she with her inbred British fear of the young,
their awful permissive speech and eating habits,
her policeman-father bringing up kids strictly,
not like ours – echoing neighbours' complaints.
And what they were saying about them all over town,
waiting by the school gates. She took you aside,
passed it all on. 'What they need is Discipline.
He's hopeless.' In other words – Their Mother.

You believed it.
How could you not believe it?
All that expense just so you could hear it –
'Fathers can't cope. Especially *him*.
The children need you. You!'

Music to you.

And this was your only fault in this story,
allowing this woman to tell you your business,
this woman to whom, otherwise,
you would never have given the time of day.
I didn't need the bank manager's advice.

I knew the point against her was being proved,
that her white-haired motherly British judgements
would be taken down and not put back,
that our life was seeing the end of Brenda.
But two hundred and forty five miles apart,
your problem wasn't solved – how to be a mother
and not a mother – how to make these ends meet.

Your Day Came

When our days crashed into new currents
tugging and struggling between us,
I tried to live in your singing, in your laugh,
in your voice on the phone to somebody else.
'I want another story,' you were explaining.
'Different. Prolific. This one's dead.'

You owned all our past. All my future.
To be rid of it
you would accept even the lowest offer.
You were almost ready to give it away.
Through the phone, its cord stretched
from hall to a closed-door room –
Who are you speaking to now?
Who's paying? Who's called who from where?

And when you cuddled the children in their beds,
laughed with them in the mornings, and I listened,
'Gradually' was the word I had in mind –
that all this would have to stop, but 'gradually'. Gradually

the house itself would find less room for you,
you less room for it –
each day getting used to itself, each week,
month, living in it, living without
your voice day by day
in what we do, say –
that since days show us who we are,
you will leap, gradually, into your own.

The Common Task

Who do they see by the sink when they come home?
Against whose rules ditching skateboards,
bags of books, kit, junk in the hall?
No clay pot in the garden without fag-end.
Never any corner without its sock.
Telling the time by what's gone off in the fridge.
Walking the timeless aisles of supermarkets.
Writing sick-notes, seeing washing done.
Inventing rules for dishes, dope – No Dope,
stay-over guests and length of stay of guests,
yes then no then yes, and use of the car, the phone,
money, standing unmarked in constant request-field,
waking up to the youth of the town breathing
in every room, the house chirping. Who in his right mind?

Mr M's House

A little democracy
in which people vote with their needs and feet,
socks that match, shirts for school,
who likes what to eat –
and duty rotas – getting half the necessities done at least.
'Can X stay for tea?' shouted out in hearing of X
so that No's no answer, 'drive X home?'
The only place they want to belong to is home,
extending the privilege, every other child
in town recruited, who seems to like it too –
Mr M's house.

So were he to write the song of himself
he would begin with this house, these voices,
these children, this music, his friends, their friends,
a little world extending the length of the garden,
down to the fish in the river, the boys fishing,
the girls painting the bathroom aquatic colours.
And he would like to include you too,
should you choose, but you don't,

you are just for the children, not for the house.
Not for Mr M.
Nor do you like being treated as they treat him –
someone who's just there, just a provider
of care, food, intelligence, love when required,
not when not required.

By your car door it isn't just goodbyes you hear
but politics – ties untied. The politics
of who cooks, who cleans, who eats,
who eats with who. You are an older story.

And besides, this is Mr M's house.
You've no place,
you don't even have a voice.
You expect to be treated better than
put-upon, poor, pathetic Mr M,
so many children he doesn't know what to do,
shoes strewn around everywhere.

Music also strewn around everywhere.
You have begun to sense their life
is not where you are or will be.
You have approached this point before your time,
one which Mr M will reach eventually –
that they are themselves, that this is freedom,
that this is their house,
here by consent and need and a little democracy,
strengthening their departure – for they'll leave,
sure enough they'll leave Mr M too –
this house their safe passage.

The Lake

Now it's night you wait in the reeds
with your bit of white floating crust among swirls,
tremors, lips, the seething
of invisible fins, the surface you are reading –
a primer without rules, except you know them,
only you know them.

From before the sun rose
to after it set we've been here
and you've hardly noticed clouds flying past,
or a plane high up in the heat somersaulting.
All your flow and somersault is with a line.

I watch your calm profile among the reeds,
fifteen, slim as a reed but growing, growing
invisibly, everything irrelevant but your fishing,
your day, the silence of your performance,
a dancer who stands still and is simply alert.

Between you and your bronze gold god, nothing distracts.
The perfect metal cast
of the thing you've imagined,
from sightreading to the delivered finish,
appears like one dreamed sleepwalking act.
You are in it even after we leave and are talking about it.

And the carp too are extravagant.
All day you've been listening
for these mouths,
waiting for their idiom to shift.
The cool of the set sun moves them about,

and when I'm standing by you with our net,
I'm not the one involved
with the line's weaving unnerved thinness
through which fish after fish express their weight,
rush to be free of it, to be again
an invisible fold of water.

I'm not the one. I'm just nearby,
watching with you while they exert
strengths nothing can simulate or pretend.
Nothing else has this convulsed, desperate
sudden pressure, or is the sum of the day's heat –
trees, cornfields, colours,
darkness soft as the moon that floats like bread.

Single Parent

Hearing what my colleagues worry about,
being who I am is so much easier.
No one talks of closing this family down.
No one talks, or not in our house,
about quality, curriculum solvency,
skill-oriented aims, learning outcomes,
recruitment drives, value for money,
not even occasionally 'sabbaticals'.

There aren't any. And the managers – us –
don't deliberately fail to minute items,
don't minute any items at all,
don't decide on items of major consequence
nobody gets to know about till later,
don't publish the outcome of their discussions
in some office-speak of ultimate secrecy,
don't even meet, except for one or two talks
each month on the phone.

'Your tea's in the oven, wash everything up,
cuddle the cat, (feed it first),
don't make a noise if you're late
and I'm asleep when you come in,
and switch off lights – love M' works ok here.
Sorting the gist's easier than running a faculty.

So give me a house where meetings
are in constant consultation,
constant ferment, all intellectual wars
wholly admitted, where the slop bucket's
not dressed up as 'interim appraisal',
'mission statement', 'adopting
positive strategies towards change',
or the menu's twelve months in advance.

Nor do we have a problem about recruitment.
Under every bed there's another bed.
Under that another. We are equipped.
I think work could learn a lot from home –
trying to get things done by the surest means,
which is that the reason too must please,
listening to them, learning that if things
go wrong it's probably my fault.

Words – Happenings

Words on screen, on a page,
in mid-sentence,
waiting for the event, the decisive
judgement, public faces in space
turning each way
for the star of the field,
the forecast heat-wave –
after the string of storms.

But the air's unclear.
We remain continuously
in good voice – nothing to say,
drinking our Meia Encosta, 1999 –
one countdown melting into another,
one wave in another, so that events
seem a thing of the past –

What's the point
of the subject of any sentence
if there's no verb?
Even when there is – *They scored.*
She won a million. A million
perished. Half a million were lost.
We are in the grip of the melting ice.
When it happens, why does it not transpire?

Anaesthetised by long anticipation.
Corralled from the leaping beast.

Imagine –
His child is killed. They're evicted.
A donkey and a rhinoceros fall in love.
Her husband's arrested for loitering.

Before it happens, it's impossible
to be inside the skin of yourself in love,
arrested, donkeylike, bereaved. You feel it
in the skin of the event, nowhere else –

magic, terror, transformation, loss –
how can we be in him or she in us
unless there are words. Sometimes
there are words and sometimes
sounds, a voice, music – sometimes crying
fragments of strings of sounds.

Mile End Opera

The man with whiskers of ponytail hair
growing out of the back of his shaved skull,
the woman with the Anna Ford face,
catacombed under London with other strangers.
Cornered, like prison visitors.
Swaying with the machinery.
Also a boy and girl – he's black, she's white.

Beautiful black and white.
He's telling her about his college courses.
Things he likes. She's telling him about her.
They are directing such smiles at each other
every one is a hit,
so that everyone in this carriage seems happier,
a shade less absent. People are listening.

Even Anna Ford is feeling distinct.
Even the shaved/unshaved head is alert.
This girl's voice is luminous with this boy.
Whatever she's saying to him she can't stop.
Just listening, just looking at her
is becoming something phenomenal to him.
And, if she's seen that smile – which she has –

she must know what the audience also knows –
that it's real, that these two are somehow
going to get off at the same stop,
that they've only just met but... what the hell...
This is it! Though they don't know it
we're all shouting for them, leaning towards them,
giving them space, swaying together,

silently wishing them things which in ourselves
we never knew,
or once or twice have known.
'This is it. Do it. Go for it',
fisting the air for them in a whole Yes!
The train stops, he gets up, goes, he's gone.
She sits staring into the walls of London.

A Balinese Mask

You gave me this for my American birthday.
Carved wood painted dazzling white.
Chin, teeth, lips, cheekbones stretched
into a permanent face-altering smile.

That was the end of March, and for yours,
four days later, I bought you a poster,
the image of an art deco hotel – Miami Beach –
a blonde with a man walking towards a convertible.
Man, woman, hotel-front, shades and car
movie style in silkscreen monocolour.

Obviously we both had a taste for shape,
simplicity, yet your present to me
was the more powerful.
Instead of something flickering in one corner,
this smile carved its whole face. It was ecstatic.
Wouldn't release either of us one bit
from the noise and stretch of it.

It's years now since you retrieved your present,
while this mask still hangs here in my house.
A souvenir – but of what? Part of a life?
How much has been carved out by this smile?
This permanent pain-shaped shout of joy?

I don't know what it was to the people of Bali,
worn for what carnival or ceremony,
so clearly a smile – angled another way
a suffering face. Yet when I look
at our daughter now, at our son,
under my skin the smile feels its way back.

Amazonas

Straight up out of the Pacific
grooves of rock that peak the clouds with ice
splinter into rivers running East.
Cloud-forests melting in July,
the Amazon at its source,
jungle of island-fringes a horizon
dividing water and sky: two azures,
evolving soft ephemera of trees
through which monkeys crash, birds cry out,
howls liquefy, great white egrets
coil downward into extreme sculpture.
Here is where the river begins to move
headlong at terrible speed
into the earth.

Thrilling with Andes snow
delivering rainclouds, fruit, vines, water,
the vast drainage of Amazon seeks every outlet
inlet and lake, and moves through it
sometimes will not move
sometimes likes to drift in a still depth fringed
by insect-floating growth, peacock fish
slothlike green canopies of trees.
But will reach salt water.
Dying into the earth's future.
Amazonas – living with its trees a few million years
together in their best of times secretly.

Alert to floating damage, torn-off roots
the shaman steers crouched,
a human rudder,
then in a liquid wilderness of glints
steering us through needles of black palm,

knowing where the simple secrets grow
trance-inducing vines,
eyes like beetles running among leaves
where trees flower –

So that night we drank his drug of bark
growing in our ears the drumming
of millions of insects, nightjars, frogs,
seemed like a city's steady traffic hum
heard from an open skylight or a street,
all sound vacuumed from the trees
into a jet of planet-circling air,
as over mountains our small plane
broke through the seal of mist
into a wide entrance of green heat,
rivers coiled like empty asphalt tracks.

Father and son
– steering words,
moving upstream.
Alligator eyes
caught red in flash-beams in the reeds.
Upstream to the coolness of our camp.
The moment being given to us again –
that we were here and saw the rim of the galaxy,
a shapely arc,
huts on the shores,
after-sunset handling of nets,
all of it blowing through us gusts of elation,
sharp joy –
the Milky Way,
slant of the Southern Cross,
riding in that boat against the wind.

Christmas Day

Not far from the age your mother was
the year I met her – summer of '77,
you're in a Castro cafe called 'The Cafe'
December '99 – writing your diary,
e-mailing chunks home –
'Random people stop and chat to us
wearing such bright colours.
You wouldn't find English families
walking around in the same T-shirt and caps.
It's bizarre. I feel like a piece of driftwood,
as in the Travis song. This time I'm here
no longer in the wake of my parents.
I've broken off from the tree
and am just floating. It feels good.'
Then from Santa Barbara a week later –
'It's like discovering new, rare breeds.
Richard, the witty, black dude
who smokes weed through a pipe.
The oldish French woman I suddenly
started dancing with at breakfast.
The woman in shades and a scarf who walked around
like she was some kind of celebrity in hiding.
Danny the old guy who cooks and drinks much vodka.
John the good-looking guy with painful stubble.'
And then later –
'Venice Beach on a Sunday is just like Golden Gate Park
but there are far and many more mad people per square metre.
And you can get a beach massage for only $5.
I hope I don't feel family-sick (note that it won't be
homesick, England is miserable) on Christmas Day.'
What shall I say? Some words really do it,
and you've found them. These are yours,
next to mine and worlds away

from puddles, streets, December, work,
yet who could be more pleased to hear them,
feel them shine across our dark.
Easy as speech they crash out with you,
wake when you wake,
colouring your country of the sun.